Journey to Thank You

RENEE MORAN

DEDICATION

To my children you have given me endless encouragement,
insight, inspiration, always believed in me and the possibility
of reaching my potential.

Thank you for all the beauty, balance and blessings you share
with me.

TABLE OF CONTENTS

PREFACE

Why Thank YOU?

Simple, one day I said to myself I should be grateful for my life. After all my life is a gift. Coming into this world we don't know the time we have or what lessons we need to learn. Each day brings the hope for tomorrow and asks us to discover our true purpose.

Reflecting on my life, I realized each fragment of time has provided me with something, be it a lesson or an experience. With each task there was a person I could associate with aiding in my journey. All these people in my life assisted me in becoming who I am. With each person there was a relationship. Those relationships coupled with the moments of time are the threads that make up the fabric of my life.

With such a realization I wanted to express my thankfulness and gratitude to those individuals. Because my life would not be what it is if not for those shared instances.

PART 1
MAKING MOMENTS MATTER

RENEE MORAN

Welcome to Why

Historically, people merely settle into life. They find themselves going to work and moving forward but stopping for brief celebrations of birthdays, holidays and anniversaries while watching time pass. They move forward in life without paying full attention to the moments that matter.

Growing up as the eldest child in a family of four, milestone-markers were not prevalent. Celebrations were major holidays and birthdays. I finished up my education, married and had children. As a mother, I chose to celebrate every moment, focusing on the time markers in life...the first words, the first steps and then the glorious first birthday. This led into half birthdays, dog birthdays, first day of school, promotions, graduations and you name it, I celebrated life.

On my husband's 40th birthday, there was plenty of fanfare, a trip to Las Vegas, a helicopter ride through the Grand Canyon, shows, dinners and special time together. For me, this trip didn't turn out as I had hoped. We returned home to life as usual or in terms I've come to reference "How it's supposed to be."

The following morning, standing in the shower, at 38 years of age, I took inventory of my life. I asked myself how do I stack up with society, family expectations, you know, the "How life is supposed to be." I continued, "Is this how I expected my life to be? Am I successful? Am I happy? What does any of that even mean to me?" My internal examination taught me - to society I looked successful having the marriage, ability to stay home and parent our two children, one dog, one cat, the status home, car and ability to travel the world. As far as my family's expectation I not only met I exceeded in that department. The true test was me and my heart. Sadly, that discovery I had to keep to myself. In this moment of time I felt an internal shift in my life that was unexplainable. I put myself on watch in a holding pattern giving myself 2-year time markers to feel change.

Flash forward two years; it was my 40th birthday. I woke up to cards and a box of chocolates from my children. There was no acknowledgment from my husband. Another day in life heading to work. I went home for lunch to a grocery store bouquet of flowers left on the table. I was alone, no fanfare, no celebration just another day in the week. My heart felt as if it was slowly shriveling up. I keep going for everything around me rather than for myself.

Another 2 years later in celebration of my 20th wedding anniversary rather than a shift my world began to shake. As I reflected on my life to that point in time, I noticed several things: my children cared more about me and my feelings than my husband. I had always hoped for a life shared not a life lived separately waiting on someone else, as a wife I existed but didn't matter. My job was just that a job. Not a career, not my own business, simply someplace to go to collect a paycheck to live. I didn't matter there. In fact, I was just given notice of reduction in work force. As far as happiness well that appeared as an illusion. I was to a point where I didn't want to live. I was fighting a daily mental battle with myself and harbored thoughts of suicide. With a grim outlook I decided to stop protecting everyone and made drastic changes.

It had been 4 years since I inventoried my life. At 42, the shaking in my world gave way to a full-blown quake and crumble. I made the toughest decision of my life and divorced my husband of 22 years. I found myself without the support of a husband, searching for a new home, 2 teenage children, in need of job and a faint idea of what made me happy. With what felt like a limited direction and a world of possibilities, I began my path of awakening.

For the next several years I dug in. Helped my children through college, stuck with a job to provide for health benefits and ability to support us. During these years there was no self-fulfillment, yet I felt my grounding grow. I took vacation days to travel in hopes that seeing the diversity in the world would provide me with some form of inspiration for my own life. I took pictures in my travels to display in my environments at home and at work to remind me of the courage to change, how each adventure filled my soul and saw it all as an investment in myself.

At 49 years young starring down the barrel of the upcoming milestone birthday the big 5-0. I decided to take inventory of my life to listen, follow my heart and discover my purpose. I realized our heart is our life's compass. For all the years I truly listened it guided me to be me. Wanting to make a difference in the lives of all those people that had touched mine in the last 50 years I decided to start my passion project.

I called it "Making Moments Matter" and the goal was to send a personalized photographic notecard each day for 365 days. Yes, 1 year to people that had an impact on my life. To thank them for the memory I recalled, lesson I learned, joy and happiness shared which not only lasted a lifetime but lent a hand to uncover the person I am today and whom I'm growing into for tomorrow.

The Process

I began my search for the why by listing people, relatives, friends and colleagues who had influenced me both positively and negatively. As I read over the list it was as if each person's name evoked a vivid memory, a moment in my life that held some significance for me. What I came to realize was that these moments and people touched my heart. And I wanted to write them a letter thanking them from my heart. That was the day I realized our hearts truly do connect us all.

I developed a spread sheet including the person's name, address, where I knew them from, the date I wrote them the notecard and the effect the notecard had on them if they told me. My list grew to 365 people. I remember an old commercial when I was growing up for a hair product that would double the number of friends and the tag line was "and you tell two friends and so on and so on." That was my idea to pay it forward. All 365 people received a photographic card from me. Along with the card I sent a "Statement Sheet" on why moments matter, a self-addressed stamped note card I asked them to send onto someone else. Lastly, I asked for them to send me an email if doing this touched them in some meaningful way.

In an age of computers, email, texting and social media, my small novel idea of sitting down writing a notecard using a pen and paper seemed old fashioned. The intent was to be personal, to make each recipient feel how much they mattered in the life of another. I crafted each card using a photograph I had taken along my travels. This was my small way of sharing the world I'd captured with them.

The Statement Sheet

The statement sheet was my way of translating the project, allowing the recipient to not only understand the process but also my hope that they would continue the mission. I asked the recipient to take a moment to reflect on their life, send the card they received to someone that may have shared a meaningful moment with them and to pass along the feelings and thoughts they felt to that person. My hope was that they were all filled with good intentions.

I came up with the idea to include a small note – statement sheet. Fashioned on a colorful 5 ½" x 11" sheet of paper that read:

Mission: Making Moments Matter

There are so many moments that make up our lives. Memories we have shared with family, friends and co-workers to brief encounters with people we've never met again. What if you took a few minutes in your day to recall one of those people in your life that shared a moment with you whether it be good, bad, happy or sad and sent them a short note expressing your appreciation, joy or laughter; acknowledging that time spent and how it affected your life. How that moment with that person, or event has become part of your dash in life. Its these moments that all seem to interconnect us one to another.

Then if in turn that person was to share one of their memorable moments and before you know it we may be creating a movement of gratitude, realizing we all impact each other in ways both big and small.

I set my mission to send one note each day for a year to people in my life past and present recalling a shared moment. With the hope of impacting their day in a positive way; understanding that they will forever be part of the fabric of my life and I am thankful to have shared time with them.

I challenge you to use the enclosed stamped note card and send it to the person that comes to your mind that you shared a meaningful moment with.

Then when you have spare time email me at: kreativekidz@hotmail.com and express how it felt to receive the note, your feelings after reading it and of course if you decided to continue moving the mission forward.

The Evolution

I wrote one card a day for an entire year. As I did this, every moment, memory or thought I shared with someone came into focus. I sat down and journaled to each person. I wrote a personal note that expressed a joyful moment of laughter, what they had taught, showed or shared with me, something I learned from them or thanking them for their presence in my life.

As I looked at my photo on each photographic card, it was as if I knew who was to receive it. Whether it was to share a destination, artistic intent, or a moment I thought they could relate to in the picture. Sadly, I never documented which photos I sent to which recipients. The pictures, metaphorically, were merely the icing on the cake. After writing the card I enclosed a self-addressed notecard and mission statement for the project to be moved forward.

Coming from a marketing / advertising background I knew statistically on average 10% of cards I sent out would be returned. I was also well aware I might not hear from many of the recipients on the impact of this gesture. I thought to some recipients this would be a "blast from the past," for other recipients they may have preferred to not hear from me, and still others would think of it as a sign of kindness shared. The funny thing was none of that mattered. It was as if I was guided on this mission for reasons greater than myself and I was going to see it through and then examine the outcome.

Working Environment

The dining room table became mission control. My make-shift desk held my laptop, box of photos, a year's supply of empty photocards, notecards I had stashed over the years, statement sheets, pens, post-its and stamps.

I carried a small journal with me because this project began in a very organic way. It seemed there was a point in each day when I was reminded of a shared moment with someone. I'd open my journal and write myself a note of the recalled event, person or feeling to reflect on later.

Every day I would come home from work, feed the cat, make dinner and compile the thoughts I had journaled. I'd sit at the dining room table look through my photos and choose the one. After inserting the picture into the photocard, with pen in hand I wrote a heartfelt memory or shared moment to the daily recipient. Next, I recorded on the spreadsheet the recipient along with the date card was mailed. This provided me with the ability to track the project's progress.

Then the assembly began. I then folded the statement

sheet around a self-addressed stamped notecard placed it in my photocard and slid all the items into the envelope. I addressed the envelope to the daily recipient, adhered the stamp in top righthand corner and it was ready for its journey. Then the next morning into the mailbox it went, flag up awaiting pick-up and delivery.

I found in my working environment that the supply of pictures and notecards saved through the years was endless. I had enough photocard holders and statement sheets to see the project through the year. When I began this undertaking, I had several booklets of "Forever" stamps which were fine for the enclosed notecards. However, I came to discover the photocards, between their size and weight with enclosures required additional postage as did any international cards. Therefore, I found myself visiting the post office more frequently than initially expected.

To my surprise the USPS stamp selection matches the diversity of our world. The varieties range from cultural holidays, seasonal, landscape, famous people from presidents, musicians, actors, historical figures, astronauts to sports, foods, desserts, fruits, flowers, cartoon characters, toys the choices are endless. The post office even has what they call "Stamp it Forward" semi-postal stamps where part of the funds of the stamp is contributed to the causes you care about such as Breast Cancer and Alzheimer's. Throughout the year as I required more postage, I took advantage of using all varieties as to me the stamp was the final artistic stroke that detailed my photographic notecard presentation.

Pictures and Travel

One of the ideas I had during this process was to use my many photos taken throughout my travels. You see, for me, as I look through the camera lenses to take a photograph, I think…wow how blessed am I to be here capturing this moment! With that thought it seemed only normal for me to share my photos and create photographic cards.

While choosing the photographs for the cards I came across this quote:

"The essence of all beautiful art, all great art is gratitude." ~Friederich Nietzsche

As I read that quote, I said to myself, to me these are simply my photos nothing fabulous, not sure you can say art, yet beautiful to me. Therefore, I'm using them to share in this project of thankfulness and gratitude…this is the quintessential meaning of kismet.

The sharing of my photos of areas I've visited was a modest way for me to share the beauty of the world I've been able to encounter, in hopes that a glimpse of my experiences would resonate with the recipient of the card.

The following statements presented themselves to me evoking a feeling that tied into this project.

- Memories made together last a lifetime
- One travels not to escape life but for life not to escape us
- An investment in travel is an investment in yourself
- Jobs fill your pocket, adventures fill your soul
- Travel is never a matter of money but of courage

These statements enable me to associate their essence with not only this project but with my passion for it.

Sending one of my pictures with each note enabled me to share my passion for life, travel, connecting spirit with thankfulness and gratitude to every recipient.

Family...Friend...Adventure

Family First

I was raised to believe that family comes first. They are the ones who support you, come to your rescue, dig in next to you when times are tough and stick with you always. I was seven when our family went through a divorce. Under our roof lived myself, my mom, my brother, two sisters along with a multitude of pets from furry babies to fish and birds. However, our family seemed so much larger. Growing up Italian means everyone is family. When you marry your spouse's family, they are family and the in-law's family is family. As one's life grows, so does their family. After being married I gained additional family with whom I shared moments for more than 20 years.

I realize that there are people in this world that believe family is only blood related – to me, that is a very archaic vantage point. Family is constantly increasing in size. After all those are the people that touch your life & heart give you the memories that fill you. Even our neighbors are like our extended family sharing things from a cup of sugar, to watching pets when they were out of town to those celebratory life moments like holidays, anniversaries and birthdays.

Growing up, all celebrations meant a house full, sometimes standing room only. It all made for some memorable moments. Those moments seem to flood my memory banks. I can recall spending time with my cousins, having water balloon fights in the bedroom hallway and playing wiffleball after holiday dinners in the driveway. I remember my grandfather sitting in his chair reading the newspaper after work telling us the importance of an education and my brother at the age of 6 taking my sister in the car thinking they could go get pizza and watching the car roll backwards into the street. I still see the image of the women that lived behind my grandmother who would visit every Friday night to play cards, share recipes, and catch up on family events. Most memories were in, what now seems a more innocent time of life, yet still has its place to allow me to acknowledge were I've been and how far I've come. Now it's my time to make it better for those next in line.

The first card in the project was sent to my mother. My mom was always my biggest supporter, encouraging me to do more and be better than her. It seemed, I was her, as she called me her $100 an hour therapist. She always needed to talk, and I was what she needed, her listener. Mom had been in ailing health the last few years suffering with heart issues and strokes. I sent her my first card so she knew in my special way I was thankful for her in my life and for all the wisdom she shared with me. As an adult, and with her recent passing, I've grown to appreciate her time in my life along with what wisdom she did provide me. The moment I sent that first card I knew it was game on. I now had a 365-day project with one goal: completion. Afterwards I would examine the process with the hope of sharing the outcomes with others.

Throughout the project I sent a card to each and every one of my family members. You name them and they received a card. My daughter, my son, ex-husband, brothers, sisters, cousins, mother, father, stepsiblings, aunt, uncle, former in-laws, neighbors, past girlfriends & boyfriends even my children's current significant others. I left no one out and a few times even wrote to the departed family members. I felt that even though they may have passed, their spirit is still out there. I wanted them to know I was thankful even though I may not have been able to express it prior to their departure.

My relationship with my biological father had its ups and downs and in the adult years it was more non-existent than ever. It was always all about him my whole life. I even sent him a card the first one I sent this man was returned.

Apparently, he changed his address unbeknownst to me. I was on a mission, so with some detective work, I obtained his current address. Again, the letter was sent back though this time it was put in a new envelope, addressed to me with no response on inside just the card I sent never opened. That, to me, spoke volumes. It just goes to show you that time and moments aren't as meaningful to everyone as they may be to you. Gratitude, like a relationship or the tango, takes two.

The most fascinating and my favorite part of sending my cards to my family was their responses. All were very meaningful to me and inspired me to continue my journey. My most meaningful card and response was soon to come.

My dad came into my life during my tough teenage years. Our family was basically my mom and us four kids for so long that having dad there was an adjustment for me. My dad's response was very touching for me. I believe the definition of dad is a man who truly touches your life, cares for you, provides for you, loves you the way you need to be loved. Through a hug, getting rid of a bad boyfriend, waiting up for you, driving to and from work or just to be your protector. Boy, he was always there when called upon for late night pick up, with no questions. My dad helped with construction projects, cheered my son at baseball games and helped my daughter battle emotions as we were going through my divorce. I'll never forget my dad's response. My cell phone rang as I was preparing dinner for me and my cat. I could see it was my mother's number.

There were many times over the years I'd see it was my mom calling and not answer the phone. So often the calls were long and emotionally draining. You know the type, checking in, a short lecture, updates on my siblings and their families, while never getting a word in myself. This time I debated answering the phone, I knew I would be going to full-fledged listening mode. When I did answer, it was my mom alright, but her tone was different and one that I rarely experienced. My mom was choked up as she explained to me that dad received my notecard and was crying. My words touched him in a way that, I guess, was very unexpected. Through all our years together, through all our times sharing memories with our family, I never actually expressed my love and gratitude and the depth of how much I cared for him. To me, and through all those years, we both knew how much he meant to me, but my notecard brought to both of us an uncontainable emotion that was both overwhelming and exactly what we both needed.

Friends & Colleagues

I have had many friends throughout my life. To me, my friends are like family as I become attached, commit to them, our friendship, unconditionally love them and our relationship. There have been friends from Sunday school in Wayne, NJ, friends I met while I was at college in Philadelphia, friends who I met at work – colleagues of course, but eventually friends.

I had been working in a school district for a few years. It was me and another woman in the office for the guidance department. One day I noticed there was a comparable position at a different school with more responsibility open within the district. My colleague said she was going to apply. After all, she had a connection in that building. She called and asked if they would put in a good word for her. Meanwhile I had applied for the position but told no one. In that moment, I thought typical it's not what you know but who you know.

When I received a call for an interview from the principal, I thought to myself, "Ok, you got this an interview with a principal, no biggie." As I entered the room there was a conference table surrounded by several stakeholders and only one empty seat. I thought the interview was a one on one. I sat in the hot seat as one by one each person asked questions. All I could do was answer to the best of my ability. I left confident in myself but unsure of outcome after all I had no connection, just me, my abilities and experience.

A few days later my co-worker was upset. Her connection

called to inform her someone else was hired. As she shared the information, I thought I tried, now all I can do is keep moving forward. To my surprise that afternoon I received the call that it was me. I got the job. Confidentiality was not only part of the job; it was who I was. I didn't speak a word to anyone until it appeared in the board minutes.

On the first day in the new position the principal reviewed her expectations of me, gave me a tour and introduced me to my new colleague named Carol. Funny thing, Carol was my former co-worker's connection and one of the stakeholders asking questions. As I began work that day one task led into another and before I knew it, I was whisking around like a tornado or as Carol put it "You're a whirling dervish."

Carol was in the later years of her position but in those few years we learned much from each other, not only as colleagues, but as friends. We walked very similar paths in life, and I was saddened when she retired and moved away.

Within the first month of my project I sent Carol a photocard. I was unsettled when I never received a response from her. One night as I was preparing to write one of my daily recipients the phone rang. Carol's name appeared on the phone screen. I picked up to hear "Where have you been?" I said, "Right here haven't moved." She said she had been sending me emails about the notecard and I never responded. I told her I never received any of her emails. First thought – oh great I could have been receiving responses for the last month and the email is blocking them. Rather than jumping into that rabbit whole I listened to my friend. She was thankful I reached out, amazed someone else saw and knew her in such a way and expressed how blessed she was with our kinship.

For me it was a moment of revelation, realizing how things happen for a reason, in the time they are meant to, connecting you to those in your life to help with your purpose. I began to ask myself those questions: Would I have met Carol if I never applied for that position? Would I have learned similar lessons or learned from her life experiences to be able to alter aspects in mine?

Think for a second. What is the meaning of a relationship? A relationship is the way in which two or more people are connected or a state of being connected. When you're in a relationship, it's an exchange of self, strength, encouragement, love, good and sometimes bad. Hopefully, you motivate the people on your path through your journey of self-discovery. In turn they help you be the best you and together you are better in each of your lives. When you experience those types of relationships in your life together you build each other to weather life's storms. Those relationships can be with family, friends or colleagues and they can last a day or a lifetime. Noticing and being thankful for them allows your connectivity to grow.

I sent a photocard to my friend Betsy. I met Betsy when our eldest children began preschool together. She grew up in the Midwest. She and her husband transferred to the east coast years earlier based on his employment. Betsy is a very down to earth person, cares about her family first, her environment and is always there to help others. Together Betsy and I shared in our children's lives being active together from school communities, scouts, exercising programs to struggles in each of our lives. I've grown to count on her endurance, resilience, and encouragement. She is a woman that will be there to help and support you no matter the circumstance. Betsy, like many people, is not open to sharing the emotionality of her life.

A few weeks after I knew I sent her a photocard she called. We were discussing details on an upcoming trip when she slid in a quick "thanks for the card I'll get around to it." I knew from Betsy that was an I love you too moment.

My mother would say its because she was from Midwest. I differ. It's not the location that makes the difference in how people react it's the environment they know, were raised in or are familiar with. I was raised to be open in all things, in touch with my emotions, spirit and to communicate in any form I could. I was told to follow my heart at a young age. That concept took me years to not only understand, but even more to listen and act on.

I sent cards to friends and colleagues and many acknowledged receiving my card. Some, giving me the response, I hoped for, would see me and cry saying "your message was so beautiful" sharing how the words touched them. From day to day, I never knew what to expect from anyone. As I started to see the effect of my notecards, it was as if this moment that I chose to share – the one that mattered to me opened emotional doors. I started to see that once I shared my memory or story, there seemed to be an emotional release for me and the recipient. The response was typically joy, grace, laughter, love, a sense of caring, thoughtfulness, understanding providing them with and acknowledgment in their life. For myself, I found inner gratitude and my "gratitude jar" was overflowing.

I didn't receive too many responses from friends and there were those that thought the idea of my "mission" was touching and they promised to propel it forward. There were others – well, for them, not so much. One friend called me to say, "yeah, got your card, thanks." Very anticlimactic. Another very close friend, told me how she read the card and it made her cry. Then, when she read it to her husband. He was speechless as well. Then there was the co-worker who seemed to hug me for forever. It's funny, I think I needed the hug that day and she seemed to need a hug too and we shared one all because of my notecard.

Of the photocards sent to childhood friends, I only received one response back. In fact, it was on the notecard I provided for them to reach out to someone who had touched their life. At first, I thought "you were supposed to send this to someone else." Soon, as I sat down to read the card, I realized that to this person, I was an important person from her past. That was an "ah-ha" moment on my journey. I had had my mission turned around on me and I was the recipient of a card and I had no idea that I had made a difference in her life. It was right then and there that I realized that other people were receiving these blessings from me, but I had, in fact, received a blessing from another. I guess that is how life truly works. As you touch someone else's life and share that they are important, they can sneak up and get you right back.

Adventure

I have grown to enjoy adventures. Small adventures like area towns and places I have never visited. I'll take adventures to get a meal or to check out the shops. Then there are those adventures that are bigger and require a long road trip or even a plane ride. For me, through all my adventures and experiences, I have a potential to gain new perspectives on life. You can see new ways you can be with and affect mankind. I've discovered in these adventurous moments, whether simple or grand, it is always our interpretation of the moment. It also gives us moments that can shape ourselves and enhance our journey.

There was the day I went to my local sandwich shop to get a sandwich for dinner. You know, one of those days you have when you don't feel like going to the grocery store and shopping for something and cooking it and you don't want a long sit-down meal at a restaurant. This one night as I was standing in the sandwich shop waiting to order a # 7 – hoagie a gentleman came in. After our polite "hello" he began to engage me, talking about a book he was reading. I didn't really want to talk but something told me not to brush this off but to really listen to what he was saying. Lucky for me, I saw this as an opportunity that this man was sharing something with me for a reason. We talked as our sandwiches were being made by the people behind the deli-style counter. Before we parted ways, I took a photo of his book's cover with my phone for easy reference. I asked him his name, told him mine and we both went our separate ways.

I decided to purchase the book and read it. Reflecting on this chance meeting allowed me a moment I otherwise may not have appreciated. Through this man's recommendation, I read a book that opened my mind and awareness and I gained a new perspective on humanity.

Two weeks had passed, and I went back to that sandwich shop asking about Melvin. My hope was to gain some insight to send him a card thanking him for that moment sharing and how his influence affected me.

The conversation went something like this...I said, "Hello, can I have a number 2, long roll, lettuce, tomato, mayonnaise on one side of bread and mustard on the other." Woman behind counter, "Sure." Myself, "Oh by the way I was in two weeks ago and met a man by the name of Melvin. Do you know him?" Woman behind the counter, "Well, which Melvin? The one that works in construction or the one that works in the piano shop?" At that moment the door opened, and a man came in leaned against the counter and said, "I'd like my usual." The woman behind the counter said, "Or this Melvin he's the original he owns the ice cream shops, you know, Melvin's Sweet Spot." In my mind I thought to myself first I was shocked a man with same name just walked into sandwich shop, second how often do you hear this name; hardly ever in my world, third for a man with the name to walk into the sandwich shop at that moment, I knew I had to reach out to the original Melvin, the one I met because this was too ironic. I said to the woman at counter, "No this isn't the Melvin." I described our encounter sharing of the book title and his views. "Oh, that's piano store Melvin; he works up the street."

Next day, I googled the piano store for the address and sent one of my cards to this man. To date I have not heard from him, but that's okay, because to me the entire experience is an example on how different people are put in our paths for different reasons and how we each accept those chance meetings is up to us.

During this year-long process, I did explore the world. I have a love of travel seeing new places, tasting new foods, learning about other cultures, capturing the beauty in all things. Whether it be moving amongst the states or traveling abroad I see the world having endless possibilities to unfold to us all.

One day on a trip to Iceland a friend and I adventured out

to see a small fishing town. It was a typical day, cold and slightly overcast the journey to the fishing town was long on roads where all you could see for miles was the beauty of Iceland from sandscapes to waterfalls, lava rock to farmland with plenty of horses and sheep scattered along the route. After several hours we entered the small town. In comparison to America there wasn't much a local gas station, school, houses some even on cliffs, a deli, two restaurants, post office, a store with everything from fishing gear and candles to kitchen utensils and gifts. As we climbed up to the light house, we could see the outer islands in that moment I acknowledged how small you are in this world we live in. As we were headed out of town, we decided to stop at one of the restaurants for lunch.

As we walked up the wooden ramp to the door, it was silent and there wasn't any hustle or bustle barely any people walking in the neighborhood on this weekday. As we entered what seemed like a renovated old house there was a serene feeling. The decor was a chartreuse green with pictures of the town draping the walls, a full banquet seat along the right side with sheep pelts adorning the chairs and tables-for-two on the left. Nothing less than cozy. There was only one other couple finishing up their meal. The waiter was the son of the owners, the food was all locally sourced and it offered a limited menu. They sat us at the table between the front desk and dessert cabinet. As we sat down glancing over the menu, I thought I don't know how this is going to be as I overheard the couple ordering dessert seeing the cabinet next to me with limited selection.

As the other couple left, it gave us time alone with the waiter, a lovely young man following in the culinary profession as generations before him. He explained the sourcing of the menu, his aspirations and presented us with a meal I will remember for a lifetime. I couldn't tell you if it was the location, the meal, or sharing the time with the waiter but the result it made in my life was so impactful that when I returned home, I sent a card filled with gratitude.

I suppose the question is then in these instances did those cards matter or make a difference? That I may never know from the recipient's standpoint. What I do know is the influence those encounters made in my life were memorable moments and I'm thankful to have had them and shared my gratitude for them.

Responses...Correspondence

Passing of Time

To my surprise I had sent cards out for nearly a month and didn't receive a response. Then I received a phone call. One of the recipients a lovely woman I worked with who called and said she had tried to send an email, but it kept getting bounced back so she decided to personally contact me. It was touching to hear how a simple card made someone feel special, appreciated, loved and that their presence mattered.

Cards went out every day each one filled with a heartfelt message of gratitude, though the responses and surprisingly the returns were few and far between.

As cards were returned, I held onto them and searched for a new address, contacting other connections to that person seeking their address or when all else failed, Google always came through. The plan was to send out the cards twice. After that, if they were returned, they would be kept in what I referred to as the "Dead File".

The question in my mind as I awaited replies was simple...Did my personal, meaningful, display of thankfulness touch a life? Was receiving the card as influential to the recipient as it was to the sender?

Responses trickled in by way of text, social media, email and good old postal service aka pony express and yes, a few were returned. However, to my surprise the amount of returns was far less than I anticipated.

Emails

It took about 3 months before I received the first email response to Making Moments Matter. I noticed the emails received mainly came from old close friends who, though we may not have been in contact recently, were the friends that we could pick right up where we left off. You know those friends in your life who reach out and at the time both your lives are busy but, you try to get together and when you do well you just relax in each other's company enjoying the time spent together, picking up right where you left off?

As I saw the subject line on the email, I slipped the communication right into a folder to read at the end of the delivery process. I can honestly say every time one did appear in the inbox, I was excited in that it gave me that push at a time I needed to keep writing and reaching out.

At the year point of the project I took a 9" x 12" envelope and put all the correspondence inside. As I was preparing for my next adventure, I sat quietly, reading each and every response.

The feeling that washed over me were nothing less than peace, joy and love. To realize a simple note made another feel special equated to a successful project.

A few of the responses were as follows:

"Thank you for the card and the memory of laughter with great people who I call my friends. I often think of that shining moment every time I see a cat!! I can still hear Cheri saying, "Oh Lord, Karen laughing relieved it wasn't her but understanding at the same time. And, you are laughing saying, Gotta Frank, Finally, let it go, it's okay. And I did, let it go! Alcohol and games do not reveal my most intelligent side. But that day and time, I never felt such acceptance! That was a Moment that Matters to me, I can let it Go and still be Accepted as cemented when the three of us met for drinks, we knew one was missing but whether we are in NJ or Texas, all of us remember and possess Making Moments Matter. Thank you for being my friend and Yes let us keep getting together for more happy, memorable, Laughter that makes making Moments Matter for each one individually and collectively." ~Barbara

"So awesome to hear from you! It truly made my day so much brighter! I feel the same, that we can always just pick up where we left off! I'm very happy for you and this journey that you're on. I will take up your challenge. I think about things like it all the time! But life just keeps moving and hurrying us along. Would love to talk sometime soon." ~Stacey

"Thank you for writing to me it was such a delightful note to receive in the crazy times we live in now." ~Sue

"I came upon your most thoughtful note and it absolutely touched my heart. You encompassed everything I try to bring to a yoga practice. Thank you from the bottom of my heart! I will for sure send the enclosed card to someone. In love, light and peace." ~Len

"Your note made my day. How could I forget a reporter writing her notes on her arm? We both had a good laugh over that scene. Can you believe that was back in 2005 (13 years ago already). Time flies. I have not forwarded a note as of yet but will." ~John

"WOW! To say your note was a surprise to receive is an understatement! I was shocked. After reading the mission statement and then to read your note was an incredibly moving experience. After 12-1/2 years for you to think of me, let alone, to write those heartfelt words was very emotional for me. I truly loved having friends over to scrapbook with. You in turn gave me a hobby I continue with today. So, thank you too, for the wonderful introduction to a hobby that allows me time to be creative and find quiet moments with new friends. Thanks for making a difference in my life.

Oh, and yes, I am carrying on the Making Moments Matter campaign! If I can make one person feel the way you made me feel with just one note, l will be ecstatic to bring them such joy!

Thank you for sharing your courage in expressing yourself to make a difference in this world." ~Karen

"When I got the letter I was excited to read what was inside, but was not expecting what was written. Your words made me so happy to read that tears actually came to my eyes... and I'm not a crier. It was so nice to get a letter on a "just because" basis that had the specific intention to spread joy and community.

I remember my first thoughts after reading the orange note about the "Making Moments Matter" mission were "Wow, she sends one note a day; that takes such dedication." and "How does she find the addresses of everyone?" When I thought about how much time and effort you must put in to sending out these notes to so many people, I was amazed.

After procrastinating for some weeks, I decided to sit down and continue the mission. I forgot how enjoyable it is to write a letter with actual pen and paper, penmanship. I love this idea and I am so happy to have been a part of it." ~Jennifer

Texts

Being a contact in any persons cell phone they were able to quickly respond and so did nearly 23 recipients with a few of the responses below.

"Thank you again for the kind card. I still have it hanging up in my office." ~Bill

"At first I thought it was a wedding invitation. I put it aside and read it to myself when I had a moment. It made me cry. Thank you" ~Lee

"That card arrived at the perfect time…I wasn't feel thing that great and it lifted my spirits. It was very meaningful." ~LuAnn

"Thank you for my card and message. It means the world to me. I think of you often. You are the inspiration that gets me through each day. Hugs." ~Diana

"I opened your letter. It brought me much happiness to know that you are ok! It made me smile to think of those same memories. It made me sad that we are not in contact more and that life gets in our way! But it is with great pleasure that I still consider you one of my best friends and you would be one of my first phone calls if I need anything! I do plan on continue the mission on a smaller scale perhaps. I don't have your energy, the time or that many people to send to! But maybe there are more than I think of as I take time to reflect on my memories. Thanks for making my day and for being you. You are, and always will be, special to me and my family!" ~Lori

"Thank you so much for the card you sent me your words meant so much to me I started crying when I was reading it, I'm grateful for you." ~Gina

"Thank you for the beautiful card. I am so touched by it. You don't receive handwritten cards any more from people and this was such a precious gift. It was also a confirmation for me that the Lord placed me for a reason. Even if it was only a season. He had a purpose." ~Katie

These responses seemed to arrive on my phone when I least expected them to; yet I must admit their timing was essential.

I'm unable to put into words how this project seemed to interconnect with my soul. On a day where I gave at work, gave to my children, gave to my friends, gave to my community and was exhausted feeling totally wiped out, I'd receive a text from a Making Moments Matter recipient. In that moment it was as if I was revitalized in spirit to continue the mission and my day. It was as if I received a boost of energy or a new energizer battery.

Social Media

I realize we live in an age where all individuals express themselves differently. Many more people are attached to their phones in our society, making social media a quick way to touch many lives. However, I look at social media and think of Andy Warhol's statement, "In the future, everyone will be world-famous for 15 minutes." Social media can be viewed then as your worst nightmare or best invention.

Either way today individuals have used this form of communication in expressing their opinions, views, pictures and so on, in hopes of having their voice heard.

In the past, I simply dabbled with social media with my children, family, friends to communicate my latest adventure or what I may be viewing, knowing full well they may be on this medium 24 / 7 where I'd rather be seeing, living within the world around me. I prefer to fill my time with gaining knowledge, experiences, and touching lives rather than seeing others' lives unfold on my cell phone screen.

In a time where people revert so frequently to social media there were only a few recipients that opened their social media apps to send a quick instant message. Honestly, it took me longer to figure out how to access the response on my phone's app. Just the same their feeling of gratuity was appreciated.

There was only 1 social media response to my cards and that was an Instagram message from my cousin Richard. In an effort to reach more people, halfway through the year I posted something about Making Moments Matter on Instagram.

There were 3 photos of the photos that reminded me of moments, with cards I was sending out and my comment was:

As we approach the halfway point of this year long mission, Making Moments Matter, I realize WHY this project began…to share a cherished memory thanking those individuals for what they taught me, how they enlightened me, or an experience that impacted my life. People come in and out of our lives everyday my hope is that anyone I affected through this process takes a moment to share with another in their own life to spread thankfulness.

Henry Wadsworth Longfellow said it best…The heart hath its own memory, like the mind, and in it are enshrined the precious keepsakes. Thank you all for giving me a lifetime of precious keepsakes.

Sure, it was a bit wordy. My follower base hasn't really moved much because of my post, but that's okay because living and interacting in the real world is far better than being attached to a device.

I used to view social media as just another way to consume my time and be disconnected from the world. However, recently after experiencing a global pandemic I see how social media does enable people to have self-expression, connect with family and friends in a way you might not otherwise be able to, as well as provide information & support from the security and comfort of your own environment.

Let's face it; we are all, if nothing else, social individuals. We are always looking to interact with like-minded people. During my self-isolation I've been fortunate to join a zoom meditation class and have taken several virtual meetings for my 9-5 position. Granted, virtual connections aren't my ideal interaction. But it does provide a sense of social interaction.

For myself, being in the presence of actual human beings, sensing their feelings and emotions and having the ability to give a hug or high five is essential. Knowing in these virtual times you can at least technically connect with likeminded people who are tackling the same frustrations has been nothing less than reassuring. I believe this form of technological communication does have its positives and negatives. As we all navigate through our current community circumstances we will rise above.

In fact, I have been using the social media platforms of Instagram, Facebook and LinkedIn to share my thoughts, optimism and gratitude as I navigate my way through gratitude in my journey thank you.

Thank you to all these resources for keeping us all connected allowing us to rise above.

Cards

The most heartfelt responses, I must admit, were the cards and letters I received. These recipients took time from their busy lives to write a note back. Interestingly only 2 of those responders used the notecard I had sent them.

I cherish each of those cards and letters as the thoughts shared exemplified each of those individual people and the fact that they stayed true to themselves or as I remember them. More so, for me, as I studied each note it was remarkable to read their interpretation of the mission, how they recalled me and their gratitude for being part of the process.

Here are a small number of clips from the cards and letters received:

"Well, whaddyaknow, you popped up again! I admire your perseverance in tracking me down. There are some people whose lives I know I've touched. Others, probably, but no feedback. However, you were a surprise, a rather pleasant one I might add. In 38 years at the office we've probably had almost as much staff turnover as the White House. I remember almost everybody but, as I am sure you have experienced, people enter your life and exit your life merely passing through. Anyway, I was flattered, even honored to know that I had such a positive influence in your life. Be well."
~ Dr. D

"You can imagine my delight and surprise at your beautiful note. It made me realize that my life mattered, not just to me but those whose life I may have touch in some way – my very own "It's a Wonderful Life" Moment." ~Cathy

"Thank you for thinking of me! Your card made my day! It is gestures like that…that get you through." ~Jayne

"There are experiences that impact our lives forever and moments that take our breath away. You my friend, are responsible for the whole package." ~ Evy

"I love this idea, but I don't think I could do one each day…365! But I do love the movement of gratuity created." ~Janice

"I think it's a beautiful thing…love it…better than just getting bills in the mail!" ~Dian

Hugs

Finally, the hugs. I knew right away if one of my colleagues, friends or neighbors received their card as their eyes were twinkly and I was greeted with a warm, hardy hug. Every time this happened, they would whisper a few words in my ear, things like, loved the card will keep it going, that card moved me I just need a hug, thank you that was such a meaningful card and for me the best one – why are you sitting at that desk and not writing.

The hugs were encapsulating filled with such emotion, intent and thankfulness. Those hugs allowed me to see for that moment that all our lives interconnect, we all need that moment of emotion and when you give into it the energy resonates into your soul. Some individuals needed to give the hug as much as I needed to receive one.

Each response made me realize from day to day, week to month throughout this past year that the fabric of our lives is woven together with the thread from all the individuals that have touched our hearts and lives. Whether they are family that stay with you a lifetime, a friend that stands by you through thick and thin, a brief encounter that enlighten your spirit, all those that have gone through each moment that touched our lives makes us who we are today. That token of thread they shared with us adds to our life allowing us to share peace, joy, hope, love, courage, strength, grace and thankfulness.

Over the years I always close any communication with Hugs. I consider it my tag line. For me it means: Hope, Unlimited Gratitude, (to your) Soul or Spirit - HUGS

We all need Hugs to be a part of our lives.

Rejections

I sent out a total of 364 cards. I know what you're thinking there are 365 days in a year. You are correct. I wrote 1 card, I knew the recipient moved in with a group of people and no matter how I tried I couldn't obtain an address. Since I had them as a contact, I texted asking for their address and it was the only time in the process I felt defeated and rejected. The text exchange was as follows:
Exchange only Rejection/Decline:
July 17, 2018 text:

Hello A, I hope this message finds you well. I was wondering what your mailing address is…where you receive mail as I have something to send you. If you would mind letting me know as I tried google search and can't find ya. Thanks

Reply 1 1/2hours later:
Hi. Thank you and I hope all is well with you too. I honestly would prefer you rather not and I do hope you can understand. Its nothing personal against you. You and your family have always been so kind to me and I thank you for that, but your daughter and I did not end on good terms and we will never

be again. I do hope you can understand. Respectfully,

My response:
I totally understand. And can say nothing else in my daughter's regard. I began a yearlong project about 200+ days ago and when someone is put on my heart having shared a moment that mattered to me, I share by sending a card to merely extend the thought and so on. I will not send the card I wrote you last night. Just know I'm thankful for many moments personally shared, I'm thankful you are happy and seem elated in life. You were always a friend and gentleman and it's been a pleasure seeing you grow into the man you are today. I only ever wish you the best. Say hello to your mom.

Response:
That is so very sweet of you. I thank you again for all you have done and for your hospitality always. I wish you the best as well and I'm very humbled by the kind words. I will pass that hello on to my mother. Best of luck with that project it sounds very eye opening. I'm grateful for the time shared too.

That rejection honestly was a blow to me and the process. It made me think how many other people are upset with receiving the cards. Then a story on the news a while back was brought to my attention. You know when you hear a card arrived 50 years after it was sent? You hear the story, see it in the media yet you think to yourself how does that happen?

As I took some time reflecting on those people whom never responded, I first thought maybe their cards were lost in that black abyss of the postal service, or more likely they 86'd – trashed the card because my influence on their life wasn't the same intent as theirs on mine.

Anyway, after examination of this one rejection I could only conclude that it rocked me. After reviewing the exchange, I resolved it wasn't me or my intent this individual was dismayed with. It was someone connected to me that we both held dear to heart. It revealed to me the effects of our soulful connections.

Discoveries

Statistics

Each response was indicative of each recipient. In the age we live in, the typical forms of communication are email or texting. Let's face it; they are both quick and easy. After all, I did state the recipient could reply to an email address regarding this mission. Yet, to my surprise of the 364 cards sent out, there were 85 responses. Which equates to 23.5% not a bad return. The responses were as follows:

Emails:	11
Text Messages:	23
Cards / Letters:	11
Hugs / Verbal:	37
Social Media:	3
Notecards Returned:	20

To my surprise 20 of my original notecards were returned. That is approximately 5.5% of the mailing, not bad. Of which 15 were sent out a second time, 5 are in what I refer to as the dead file because I can't obtain another address to forward to. The remaining 10 cards were sent out one last time. Only 1 was sent back, never opened, simply put in a new envelope with no response added the envelope in their handwriting addressed to me.

Cost vs. Profit

With any endeavor there is always a cost. Let's examine: How much did the photocards, reprinting of photos, statement sheets, notecards, postage to send photocards with enclosures and postage on notecards for recipients to send out cost?

Costs:

Supplies - The supplies included but weren't limited to photocards, pictures, statement sheets and notecards. Through my years traveling I had bins of pictures. I started by using some of those pictures. Then I purchased reprints about halfway through the project. The cost was minimal. I had a few blank photocards on hand from past endeavors and purchased a supply to sustain the project for the year. The statement sheets I printed on paper I had at home. So other than printer ink which I need regardless no associated cost. The notecards well I think we all have some kinda collection of these. Over the years one left from this set or that. You put them here or there in the house. As I cleaned house, I found a stack of them it proved to be an eclectic collection of cards. This collection honestly carried me through about three quarters of the year. I then purchased a few sets of notecards at department stores cost again low. Part of the joy was which type of notecard each recipient would receive. As they varied from blanks to happy birthday, congratulations, thank you, hooray, graphic designs, character cards that was all a whimsical aspect of the project.
Sorry to say I didn't save the receipts to provide an actual denomination. That's because the cost was never the focus of the project.

Postage - That one is two-fold as there is a cost for the card going to each recipient that included the notecard that was stamped to forward the mission. I didn't want to spare any expense as I wanted each recipient to feel they had to put no funds of their own out to pay it forward unless they chose to take this mission on after the initial notecard.

Many cards were sent within the United States of America.

However, there were also cards sent Internationally which required alternate postage options.

I could put a dollar value on the process but, I won't. You see for every dollar I put out I am blessed to say I received it 10-fold in so many other ways. This project was not about cost or profit in a dollar and cents way. This was a mission of the heart…seeing the effects of sharing thankfulness, love and light finding out deep in ones heart if the moment of remembrance or connection was still alive and will remain a part of you or if it is merely a memory to be grateful for the exchange and put it in its place and move forward.

<u>Time</u> - Now for the time it took each day for me to write a note and assemble a packet, could there be a cost associated? I'm sure there are people in the world that would argue your time is valuable, time is money and those people would say, of course – Yes. I guess if I was doing this for someone other than myself, I would expect my time to be compensated. However, this was my project, my passion and I don't think in terms of money. I began this project with a thankful heart, wanting to express thanks to those that shared in my time and journey in life.

The photocard proved as a vehicle to share my precious fragments of time and gave me joy daily from the memory, writing to mailing and receiving of responses. Time gave me thanks and thanks gave me time.

Profit:

After reviewing all the factors of this project. The supplies, postage, time one could say it sounds as if there is no profit; there may even have been a loss.

This project was never intended to be cost vs. profit relative. Let's face it. Nothing in life is FREE. This project did cost me money in supplies and postage, but nothing outrageous or beyond my means. I made sure if any of the recipients wanted to pay it forward they could but at least the first notecard was on me.

This project did teach me that everything happens in time for a reason and there are no costs are associated with time. Time is an invaluable and precious commodity. I did come to find out time will replenish you in time when you need it most.

If you had to look at this project from a financial standpoint on a profit or loss sheet it was a nominal loss.

In the end, examining cost vs. profit, listening to my heart showed me that the only word that can be associated is...PRICELESS!

Conclusion

I created a challenge for myself and was going to see it through. Believe me, there were days I thought my mailperson had to wonder, another day another card? The flag on my mailbox seemed to be up daily. After a year the flag is worn out; it can't stand up on its own any longer.

Life is an adventure sounds like a quote you'd see on Pinterest. However, you get to a point in your life where you stop, look back and realize all you've experienced, done, worked and seen. As I laid in bed in the dark one morning, I realized what a magnificent journey life is. With all the adventures I've had, world I've seen, people I've met, in that moment as old as I was, I felt like a teenager again. I was thankful for all moments and encounters, feeling blessed for each trial, tribulation and rule followed or broken. As I sat softly melted in my bed, I wondered with half my life left what marvelous moments await. Which ones will I be FORTUNATE to partake in? Which ones will IMPACT my life? Who will they be with? A daughter, son, sibling, family, colleague, friend or random person? Will that moment affect them or I, more or less?

No one knows what tomorrow will bring. We need to be thankful for each day, what it unveils to us and that what we take away is our treasured moment.

I, fortunately or unfortunately, like most people, have been through my battles, loved and lost, seen life and death and have REALIZED some people were merely meant to be in your life for a moment while others, forever. That realization could take a lifetime for someone to truly comprehend.

With this project I expected an overwhelming response. I figured if I would love to receive a note everyone would, and people would joyfully continue the mission. It wasn't long till I discovered that most people are just going through their lives. What's important to one person can make no difference to another. I discovered the responses, as long or short, that I received were from those individuals where it was a true heartfelt impact.

As I was going through a box of old photographs seeing snapshots of moments at first, I tried to see if I recognized the people in the photographs then if it was before or during my lifetime. With every picture I lifted of those individuals, I recalled and reflected on my thoughts and feelings. It was then I remembered growing up how my mother would always test us on fire prevention. She would ask if you had to leave the house because a fire started what would you take and where would you go? My response was always I'd take all the pictures and go to the neighbors. My mom would say what about your brother and sisters? I'd say, "Yeah, them too." As a young child the photographs represented a moment, I would forever be able to look back on and I figured like most kids, my siblings would always be there. It's not till you lose someone close to you that those moments really mattered. My point here is simple; take the time in your life, whether it's a card, a call or a visit to reach out to those individuals you will forever long to see, share a moment as it matters not only during that encounter. It will be a lasting memory for you to cherish.

I had a front row seat as my father was floating in and out of consciousness in his last days; for me it was like watching my mission. His body lay in that hospital bed, his eyes were closed and fluttering as whispers of words came out of his mouth. As I watched I thought of what I had heard throughout my life - before you pass on you see your life. I thought to myself, "What moments is he remembering? Who is this Dalila he is recalling? Were these meaningful moments? How did they make a difference in his life? It didn't seem as though he was struggling or having a bad dream. Was he seeing life beyond? I was captivated." It was that moment I felt the connections we truly make with the people's lives we touch deeply will forever be tethered to us. More importantly it was during these moments' that communication is so drastically different. You communicate with your heart, feelings and spirit, as the action of words is no more.

Unknown to me, this project was a gift. From the lives touched, how impactful it was to them, a revitalization to them as well as me on the precious gift of life. 365 days of sharing thankfulness gave me peace, joy, understanding, gratitude and grace.

Recently, I suffered a great loss; both my parents died a month to the day of one another. You truly don't realize your loss until those quiet moments, alone in a car, reading a card and you realize how precious a moment is.

As I was cleaning out my parents' home, I came across both the Making Moments Matter cards I sent to each of them. When they received the cards, they called and we spoke about how touching the sentiments inside were, I knew my mother had passed the card onto my sister wanting her to know how important she was in her life. I realize now I was blessed to share this experience with them. I didn't realize how impactful it would be on me and the realization that a moment, no matter how long or short matters to the person and life you touch.

I know now how inter-connected we all are, how precious life is and to fulfill not only a mission but to share it can hold a lasting effect on all.

To all the lives I reach out to touch, I've been fortunate enough to get that back tenfold.

One of my recipients said that writing card a day-- that is some undertaking, a profound statement indeed, and so telling. It was an undertaking as some days felt almost daunting but I'm thankful to have been able to do it. In the last few months I have discovered there are so many people that I continue to come in contact with and I find a calling deep in my soul to continue sending out these notecards to uplift those people that elevate me for whatever reason.

I've learned that the moment you say hello, share a story, find commonality you open yourself up not only to another but, understanding a deeper sense of yourself.

I was given a poem recently entitled: "Oh Mighty Oak" written by Kathryn Patheau. The author wrote the poem for her grandfather. As I read the passage, I reflected on Making Moments Matter…I thought of all the lives if but a moment have been touched and I felt a cascade of warmth.

When you take on a project the goal is to see it until it is finished. My hope is as I finish this book it takes on a life of its own and touches people's lives to realize in the hairiness of each day, in the hustle and bustle of the world, in the horror and tragedy to witnessing the joy of a new life we each have to stop, recalibrate our lives, focus those moment that make a difference in our lives, our families, friends or passersby because those are the moments we will come to realize affected our souls.

In the moment you don't always understand why someone was put on your path, just know we are here to live life together to support each other and weather life's storms. Each encounter be it through family, community, or random engagement was placed in your life to strengthen, motivate, provide you with a countless number of experiences, attributes or simply to let you know love is always in you, with you and lives on in the lives you touched. Each photocard with a sentiment was my gift to a recipient that prompted a difference not only in my journey in this life but theirs as well. It was just as important for me to send as it was to receive the responses. This journey to thank you was honestly the best gift I have ever given myself.

PART 2
COMPARISONS AND
EXAMINATION

RENEE MORAN

Meaning of Thankfulness

According to Cambridge Dictionary on the world wide web, this is how thankfulness reads:
Thankfulness noun UK
the feeling of being happy or grateful because of something:
I felt a deep glow of affection and thankfulness for her kindness.

When you look up thankful in the Merriam-Webster Dictionary on the internet it reads:
Thankful adjective
thank·ful | \ 'thaŋk-fəl \
Definition of thankful
1 : conscious of benefit received for what we are about to receive make us truly thankful
2 : expressive of thanks thankful service
3 : well pleased : GLAD was thankful that it didn't rain

I examined what thankfulness means to me.
When I began this endeavor, it was about the moments, the image in my mind and heart that I shared with people throughout my life. The bounce back factor for me was as I sent out these notes the effect it had on the people was thankfulness. They appreciated not only receiving the card but how the words and pictures touched their lives, or shall I go as far as to say touched their heart.
Their responses gave me the bigger gift no money could buy. Their smiles, happiness, hugs and shared moments made not only my heart runneth over but gave me hope. In a world that is constantly changing, moving at warp speed, with things happening in real time so fast this old fashioned gesture made time pause for all involved to give hope in friendship, community, compassion with our fellow man to if but for a

moment cherish that feeling to know everything will move forward. And by showing thankfulness, you allow the gates of gratitude to spring wide open. In turn, you discover under all that thankfulness is pure love.

If the only prayer you ever say in your whole life is "Thank You" that would suffice.
~Meister Eckhart (German Philosopher)

What does thankfulness or being thankful mean to you?

Meaning of Gratitude

According to Cambridge Dictionary on the world wide web, this is how gratitude reads:
Gratitude noun [U] US
/ˈɡræt̬·ɪˌtud/
a strong feeling of appreciation to someone or something for what the person has done to help you:
Many of his patients gave works of art to Dr. Klein in gratitude.

When you look up gratitude in the Merriam-Webster Dictionary on the internet it reads:
Gratitude noun
grat·i·tude | \ ˈgra-tə-ˌtüd , -ˌtyüd\
Definition of gratitude
: the state of being grateful : THANKFULNESS expressed gratitude for their support

I examined what gratitude means to me.
    Sure, this mission as I began was about thankfulness as that is the emotional component. As it progressed, I realized it also was gratitude because if it wasn't for all the people that have provided me with moments in my life experience, I wouldn't have the ability to look back, and I wouldn't be the

person I am at this point in life. Therefore, I am grateful for those moments that have helped form the me I am today.

That feeling of gratitude also affected my heart showing me all things in this life intersect and when you harness that energy along with good, positive, energy it can propel you and your spirit to doing what is best in the time you have.

Being grateful made me acknowledge all that I touch and touched me had an impact on both exchanges and changed my life. It opened me up not only to forgiveness, thankfulness, love and light but I found the beauty and balance within myself.

Gratitude is a practice we all should work on as it will help all involved feel better. If you search the internet you will see many psychological studies have been done with regard to gratitude. They note things such as: improves your sleep, promotes optimism, increases mental strength, and lower stress hormones in grateful people. Following a daily gratitude practice can reduce the effects of aging on the brain. Gratitude aids in developing more positive outlook. Merely being grateful makes you happy and being happy enhances both your mind and physical health. A simple way to share your thankfulness is with a HUG.

Many of us focus on gratitude during the holiday seasons to be thankful and share. Afterall we start our holiday season with THANKSgiving…gratitude is built into the name itself. Many people acknowledge the goodness in their lives at this time for the people and moments for which they are thankful. It's a tradition that sets a tone for a meaningful and celebratory season.

On a daily basis, gratitude can be hard to come by and even overlooked. We should look at gratitude as the fuel that circulates the good within our lives and communities. The more you put out the further you will go and receive. We all need to cultivate this practice in both good and bad times, to train ourselves to feel and practice thankfulness will make us feel better.

One of the nicest gifts you can give yourself or those

around you is gratitude. By sharing it you fill your heart and experience an abundance of joy.

For me time has passed since I began this process and there seems to be a very relevant need in our society for gratitude and thankfulness.

What does gratitude or being grateful mean to you?

Gratitude ... Attitude

Growing up, if you looked with your eyes at where I lived you would have thought - prestigious neighborhood in an up and coming suburb, they have it made. Sometimes though life is an illusion. Sure, from the outside all seemed well, but once you opened the door things changed.

Many times, growing up, we didn't have heat because mom wasn't able to pay the electric bill. When the pipes froze, we had no running water, and as my parents went through a grueling divorce there was no food on the table. I remember my mother preaching to us saying, "You should be thankful for the roof over your head, you have a bed to sleep on and there's food on the table. There are people in this world who have nothing." I would think to myself really were freezing, we ate applesauce on white bread with water for dinner. My bed was my slice of heaven; so maybe she was right. We had something, each other.

I'll never forget one night as she gathered us all in my room. It was the smallest so by moving all the mattresses into this room it stayed the warmest. She read a story to us that night that I'll never forget. I only wish I could remember the title and author. I'm not sure if the ink illustrations were in the book or just the images I created in my mind as she read the story. Nevertheless, it went something like this. There was a mother with 2 children. They lived in an apartment in the city. The mother gave the children the bed to sleep in as she slept on the floor. They had very little, but they were together. The mother was able to save up some money after paying their bills and for Christmas they were able to have a lit tree that illuminated the apartment. I realize decades later I don't recall all the specific details I once did. However, when my mother read us that story that night, our circumstances didn't seem as bad. After all, we were together. At the age of 9 is when I realized that if you can change your attitude, you can change your life.

A dear friend of mine recently opened up to me about her life's story. She is a recovering addict. She shared her tale telling me. When she was going through counseling for her drug addiction, her sponsors first words to her were, "You have to flip-it." I reacted with a puzzled look on my face. She said, "Rather than having an attitude that something is owed to you for being in your circumstances, you have to show gratitude for the circumstances you are in. In essence, flip your attitude, make it be of gratitude. What are you grateful for? Is it a new day, you're alive, you have a bed to sleep in, your health, supportive family. Get it?" I looked at her smiling and said, "Oh I get it." With this thought process as you move forward each new day, be grateful for something else. Get through one day and the next be thankful for one more.

Step one is changing your attitude to gratitude. Knowing full well there will be days the adjustment will be difficult but the longer you stick with that change will bring you closer to Step two which is gratitude to thankfulness.

Gratitude is the ability to shift your energy. Practicing gratitude allows you to freely express kindness, enables you to have a positive outlook and express understanding with others. Grateful is associated with a feeling. Thankful is associated with an action, making Thankfulness a gesture of appreciation.

Both Gratitude and Thankfulness work in tandem feeling and action. Therefore, practice sharing both thankfulness & gratitude will provide both the giver and the receiver gifts that can only be felt deep within one's soul.

How you act can change someone's day, thought or

merely provide a moment of happiness.

I may have begun with a very finite focus on a moment that mattered but in reflection these moments truly were glimpses of gratitude. Some days it took effort to keep the mission moving forward. Other days it was purposeful yet through it all each moment with ease or struggle I choose to focus on the positive. The process helped me become who I am today. I am fulfilling my life's purpose sharing my thoughts, gifts, laughter, love and light with the world one moment at a time.

I challenge you to embark on a mission / project of passion of your choosing big or small and see how it changes your life.

Ideas to aid in thankfulness or gratitude:
- → Create a gratitude journal. Take time each day acknowledging a few things you are thankful for.
- → Call a friend or family member let them know how special they are in your life.
- → Put a sign in a location you see every day like on the refrigerator, mirror in bathroom, dashboard of your car, on your computer screen with a phrase such as: What one thing are you thankful for today? This may help you keep thankfulness and gratitude present in your life.
- → Volunteer your time. You'll find helping and teaching others gives one a greater sense of fulfillment or purpose as your time that is so precious and valuable will have been well spent.
- → Perform an act of kindness: compliment someone, help an elderly person by bringing their grocery bags to their car, hold a door open, allow someone with a few items to jump ahead of you in line, any random act of kindness will not only help you but the other person as well.
- → Send a note to someone that helped you in some way.

→ Any act will raise your spirits and vibration as well as theirs.

PART 3
YEAR LONG JOURNEY OF DISCOVERY

RENEE MORAN

Sensory Connectivity

As I began this mission, through its completion of sending cards, through both my parents' deaths and starting to craft this book, my life took the scenic winding road. Discovering our connectivity for some it may be on a sensory level sight: sound, touch, taste and smell. While others may dive deeper in the pond to discover their connectivity on the levels physical, mental, emotional and spiritual.

Ask yourself, how do I connect with others? I think the basic go to response would be communication. Communication can be in an array of forms...talking on a phone where you hear a person's voice and inflection during your conversation, in person where you can see a person's reactions, expressions and body language, through more modern forms such as email and texting which I might add are very interpretive based on the receiver's current mindset and mood when reading this form of communication.

If someone were to say they just enjoyed a warm freshly baked chocolate chip cookie you might be able to connect to them through your sense of smell, taste or even touch.

On this road of discovery each turn presented a way to open my mind into another form of connectivity. I discovered that to truly know one's self, you set everything you harbor inside free. I decided to go beyond the basic connectivity of sight, sound, touch, taste and smell. I dove deep into the study of yoga, looking not only for the physical attributes of flexibility but the mental and spiritual effects of peace and calming of the mind and body. I noticed when you free yourself during savasana your body seems to melt into the earth, and you connect back to where we came nature. The peacefulness that washes over you wills the cavity of your soul and renewal embraces oneself.

I began with basic nutrition, changing my eating habits for

my health. Eating clean with plenty of water, organic produce and rearranging my protein base to keep my physical body functioning on a better level. At the same time, I've tried to maintain my exercise regimen of cardio workouts to at least 3-4 times a week. I wanted to build in weight training and more stretching but sometimes in life you realize something must give as there simply isn't enough time in a day. For me weight training and stretching don't happen as often as it should. I've come to accept my short comings and just roll with it. After all I'm healthy and happy; what more is there?

I explored meditation alone as well as guided mediation to teach myself to focus my mind to declutter my thoughts and inner mind chatter. I did this in hopes to train my attention, awareness so I could achieve emotional calm, mental clarity and ultimately connect with the divine. I've learned you have to keep your heart and mind open during your practice. In doing so you'll maintain a spirit of gratefulness. Once you reach the calm, your spirit of gratefulness-that feeling will bring you to a place of awakening of your true self.

I evoked my senses with the healing properties of essential oils. The abundance of oils and combinations are endless. From being diffused in a room to add fragrance, put on pressure points to give relief of stress, they can boost memory, be used as home cleaning products and promote wellness. For me they have provided aromatherapy as well as being an added tool awakening all my senses and spirit.

Thinking that the Hindus and Buddhists have for centuries studied the chakras, I decided to learn about them along with crystals as healing stones. The thought that life-energy connects the physical and supernatural elements of the body seemed an interesting avenue to expand.

Then there was the ancient practice of traditional Chinese medicine acupuncture. Chinese medicine practitioners believe the body has more than 2,000 acupuncture points connected by pathways. It's these pathways which create an energy flow known as Qi sounds like "chee" that is responsible for overall health. Improve the flow of Qi...improve your health.

Visual therapy for me is holding a camera in my hands. Having the ability to see beauty in the world, capture that moment and share it is invaluable. We all have photographs of unforgettable moments. Today, many of us keep them in our cell phones, some have photo albums, scrapbooks for the chronological reference of the memories and others keep them in boxes scattered throughout their domiciles. I have created scrapbooks of my children's educational years, our family years and have bins of photos when I was a local photojournalist. I have been fortunate to have a love of travel and have taken my camera along to capture beautiful landscapes, architecture, people and faraway places. I chose to share these photographic moments with all who have received a photocard from me as my way to show others the beauty of all the world.

Finally, there's sound therapy. I think as adolescents we all practiced sound therapy, we listened to the radio, records, cassette tapes for entertainment, to zone out, rebel, distract us from whatever we were experiencing at that moment or out of boredom. Nevertheless, a meaningful song came on right after a date, even a break-up or some moment in our lives and we connected with it.

Through the year's music has changed but, today we still download not only current songs but those that affect our lives. The playlist for all intent and purposes is called our favorites. Recently on my drive to work my morning community playlist included a random selection from my library the following songs: Feel This Moment, The Miracle, Suddenly I See, Just the Way You Are, This Never Happened Before, The Middle, Kodachrome, and Gone, Gone, Gone. Some of these songs challenged me to think about time, moments and the creation of this book, other songs brought me right back to a moment in time I could vividly see sharing with a person. As I thought about that person, I considered the feelings that time had on me and how the emotions of something that could have happened 8 years ago washed over me.

Another type of sound therapy also coined as vibrational medicine you hear and feel the vibration from tuning forks,

Tibetan singing bowls and music set with different MHz to move the body beyond relaxation, stimulate healing and spiritual connection.

The last year was filled with plenty of insight which allowed me to ascertain when you begin to expand your learning of life especially through your senses you recognize not only your reason for being but, how connected we are not only to each other but to a higher being. It's that interconnectivity that drives us all to do better not just for us but the next generation. So, when you consciously act with a thankful intent you start to change your environment in a positive direction not just for yourself but all those that connect with you.

Forgiveness

As this journey to thank you took hold of my life and I explored all different facets of life, beings, cultures and practices, one thing kept presenting itself to me...forgiveness. This was truly a process of self-exploration one can harbor emotional wounds. Those wounds do no good for you or your spirit-soul. You need to find a way to heal any emotional wounds to allow yourself to be all you can be and the key factor in doing so is Forgiveness.

Forgiveness provides you with your own growth and happiness. As individuals we need to acknowledge whatever happened of which we conceal any hurt, pain, anger or resentment. Most times what we hold onto harms our lives more than the offender. Therefore, we must be able to accept the past for the past knowing full well we can't change those events or actions that took place or the hearts and minds of the offender or offenders. We need to take inventory of our own soul and find the motivation to heal ourselves. Because that is all you can do. Live today for today building for a better tomorrow because tomorrow is a new day.

Through my journey to thank you as I addressed a few

cards to individuals I consciously acknowledged I harbored ill will for actions, emotions and harm. Rather than focus on that resentment I knowingly released those hurtful emotions and sent a card remembering something they shared, how it affected me in my past how I changed it in my present and thanked them for allowing me to grow into who I am today.

In order to complete writing this book I did have to intentionally forgive myself. I came to recognize I was holding myself back from mis-decisions of my past that needed to be left in the past so I could blossom today. I have not only opened my mind and heart but value that forgiveness truly frees us to live in the present.

Time

Tomorrow is not promised; neither is today, for that matter. Therefore, we should all celebrate today because, after all, isn't it the present? Be present in your day, be thankful for all you've been given and find joy in all things. Let go of the moments in the past yet be thankful for them, for what they have taught you. Don't wait on the future. As those future moments are in constant influx. Live your life intentionally knowing each moment is a gift.

When you live in the moment you achieve a sense of respect for all of the blessing life will bestow upon you. Don't put off enjoying your life; live it now.

For but a moment every day we should celebrate the things we do have in our lives that make us happy. Try not to be driven to a new challenge for what we think will make us happy but only makes us tired from chasing something that may not be attainable in the current term.

Thinking about what you do have and how it makes you happy may appear as a simple concept though it may prove to give you more satisfaction in your life and fill you with an unsurpassed joy.

A moment is but a fragment of time. When we piece our fragments together, we can see how our lives have formed.

I believe we are each given an undisclosed amount of time on this earth. In that time our goal is to discover our purpose. For some, that can be easy, while for others, it takes a while to come by and still others get so bogged down in life that they never uncover their heart's true purpose.

Let's face it. Between society, life, our family and friends tell us what is expected and what we should do. The problem is that we need to listen to our hearts. Our hearts tell us what our true purpose is.

Growing up, getting an education, building a life, career, family, home there are ideals that have been taught to us for generations. In that process we learn our lessons but what if somewhere in that scheme of things we uncover our gifts? We each are given gifts, our inner gifts and abilities that we never lose. We must learn to focus on our gifts to find our heart's purpose.

The true test is cherishing the time, enjoying the moments spent with family, seeing the beauty in the day, stopping to see the sunrise or sunset, listening to the rain or wind, have your breath taken away after an ice storm to see the calm after the storm.

As children we learn there is always calm after a storm, whether that storm is in nature or our lives. This is a perfect lesson of seeing time. What we each do with our time, how we help, guide and understand that time is constantly changing and revealed to us.

As I reflect on my life, I remember as a young girl in middle school I wanted to become a writer. I was outspoken, social, enthusiastic, and always doodling. I believe the middle school years are a turning point in your life where you are discovering your own autonomy and preparing for your future. I'll never forget the words of my 8th grade English teacher. She said, "You can't write; don't even try. Stick with your doodling."

That statement not only stuck with me but as I began my

high school and secondary education it shaped what I did. I was unsure of everything. I listen to people tell me what I should do rather than follow my heart. My inner compass had gone haywire and the arrow shook. With each shake I jumped to something else. I became a graphic designer (doodling) and a realtor (social). After several career changes, I decided to simply build a family. Needing more, I became a photojournalist for a local newspaper. I loved that job, until my then husband said I wasn't making enough money doing it and I needed a real job.

I have never been one to focus on the money. I was raised to be happy and follow my heart. I had gotten so off balance it took a true awakening. I saw time passing, unsure how to balance things out I gave all my concerns to God. I asked if I make it through, give me the strength to move forward on my correct path, a restart if you will.

That restart was the storm in my life, a divorce, broken family, a job to pay the bills and health insurance but no purpose other than my children. With each new day something new was revealed to me the acceptance of the sunrise, started making moments matter, touching others' lives, giving hope and thankfulness.

As I write this book, I have come to realize this is my purpose, my calm after the storm. It is to share with you that maybe somewhere in these words your heart speaks, you listen, acknowledge your gifts and fulfill your purpose.

The Link between Thankfulness and Wellness

This all began as a thought; to merely share my thankfulness with those that have touched my life. Through the process I found how intertwined our lives truly are. Thankfulness is a form of a drug called positivity. It fills our emotional bank with love, joy, and peace, which in turn, allows us to not only shine inside us brighter, but we then reflect that onto others.

Those emotions and feelings ward off diseases that go along with negativity. The less negativity we hold in our entire bodies, the better our being will be.

We are all bodies of matter on this planet we call Earth on a daily discovery not only of the meaning of life, health and happiness, but seek a better understanding of self and our place in the universe.

We discover the diversity of cultures, see not only the differences but similarities of us all. As we maintain a healthy lifestyle through nutrition, sleep, exercise, meditation, yoga, and other practices our physical body in conjunction with our mental and spiritual bodies are optimized.

My finding was by sharing thankfulness I found my spirit was reactivated, allowing me to open up and flourish in all areas of my life on this Earth.

Findings

When I began receiving the responses and hugs it was not only motivation to continue; in its own way these moments of thankfulness expanded my emotional, mental, physical and spiritual connection.

These were feelings that going through your everyday life you don't always get the opportunity to encounter. Let's face it, a typical person's day is to get up, eat to nourish your body and provide you energy for your day, you go to work that you may or may not enjoy to simply earn a paycheck to sustain you and your family in this life. That process seems to be on repeat cycle - day after day, month after month, and year after year. Sure, you may have a holiday, vacation or sick day thrown in that mix to offset yourself but, truthfully this is what we've all come to live.

Living this way, we seem to neglect our spiritual side, disengage our emotions, get mentally blocked and all of this together takes a toll on our physical body whichpays the price.

Yes, today society has us more alert to eating healthier, exercising, how many steps did you take today? We are more aware of emotional and mental illness, in creating a lifestyle for ourselves and families to better adapt. Yet at the same time we are so connected to an electronic device we forget how to carry on a conversation with an actual person in real life in real time. Our kids don't run around the neighborhood and play till dark. That is no longer the world we live in and that is disheartening.

The photocards that were sent out for Making Moments Matter were sent with the intent of a personal connection. They were handwritten which conjured a feeling, using words that came from the heart and communicated an experience or memory, on a photocard which you felt the cardstock a small treasure you could keep in sight. It was not a tweet, text or chat on a backlit device that is cold and lacking emotionality.

I discovered that with every photocard I sent out for Making Moments Matter it seemed to add more appreciation to my heart, soul and drive to experience a new day. The daily grind became just a job, but the photocards felt like my purpose. A purpose to touch a life one day at a time to make them know they matter. Because I believe once you're exposed to knowing you matter, your heart is filled with a peace and joy that not only affects you mentally, but, emotionally, physically and spiritually as well. Some days I felt like that line in the movie The Grinch, "his heart grew three sizes bigger that day."

I started to recognize there was more to the moments of memories, more than what I had learned and take on my journey through life. I realized that through all this exploration and discovery there is a link between thankfulness, light and love. Our thankfulness builds up our light, our light allows us to shine and become a beacon to others together and the thankfulness and light build up our factor of love. It is believed that the more light one holds the more beauty they spread throughout the world. The light each individual spreads in actuality is the power of love.

Effects of Love

Many years ago, my mother-in-law gave me a gift. I can't recall what the occasion was, but I've kept that gift for more than 30 years. I have it hanging in a place I see often above my dryer. It's a modest frame with a print inside that looks like a watercolor hearts in each heart reads: Love is...there are a three squares across and three squares down totaling nine Love is...statements. Within each of those the individual squares it reads: Love is...if I'm not mistaken that is from the Bible 1 Corinthians 13: 4-5: "Love is patient, love is kind. It does not envy, it does not boast, it is not proud. It does not dishonor others, it is not self-seeking, it is not easily angered, it keeps no record of wrongs. The print is not verbatim of the Bible verse rather it reads: Love is patient, Love is kind, Love does not envy, Love does not boast, Love is not proud, Love is not rude, Love always trusts, Love always hopes, Love never fails.

When I read that print, I'm reminded the strength of love. After loss, no matter how much love you have around you and within you, love seems like a figment of your imagination. As I was discovering all the ways to find peace and thankfulness in the last year I stumbled back to that print and love.

One morning after visiting with a friend, I found myself at a stop sign in the middle of the road. To my right was a small farm stand. With no one behind me, I paused my travel to review the stand. It was quite an elaborate set up with pumpkins on a flatbed trailer, there were cornstalks on either end, wood baskets filled with gourds, squashes, mums and a small wooden like cabin that only 2 adults could stand in with shelving that held homemade jams, jellies, a mini frig with fresh eggs, fresh cut sunflowers and a few handmade items. I pulled over found a pumpkin or two for the upcoming harvest season, took a few photos of the beauty and stepped into the small cabin like area to put my money in the red metal box. It was then I saw a wood sign painted on the front said Love Heals and another that read Love is Patient.

The following week in meditation the following phrase presented itself to me and has now become my mantra…Love Lives On. To me this means no matter what you do, who you connect with if you are blessed enough to share love in your spirit-soul it will live with you for all eternity.

When my children were young, I would always say "I know what you're doing because I'm always with you." My place is in your heart. Even when I'm not around or have left this life I will be with you because love is what holds us together. I've told each of them wherever life takes them send me love, call upon me so I can share in their life's occurrences with them.

Love is the thread in the fabric of all our lives we freely give and receive that binds us together. Once that resounds within you, your life lessons level up.

PART 4
A CELEBRATION AND CHALLENGE

JOURNEY TO THANK YOU

Thankfulness & Wellness Celebration

My thought process was simple. Thankfulness and wellness are interconnected. After all this inter reflection, discovery and awareness I decided to host a thankfulness & wellness event to share my newly adopted philosophies with those I felt closest to, my inner circle...family and friends to let them know I'm thankful they are part of my life.

In my old-fashioned manor, I created an invitation sent it to the 20 people that have been most present in my life over the last year. These are people who stood by me in times of trouble and joy, that helped me, protected me, and inspired me. They are people who, no questions asked, in an instant would be there for me as I would for them.

With planning any event you realize not everyone will attend and that's okay. Of the 20 invites sent out only 7 people were able to join me.

That in itself for me was telling as if you google the meaning of the number 7 you find out that 7 is a highly spiritual number, positive things are flowing freely toward you. This number is associated with intuition, inner wisdom and deep inward knowing, or in my terms IRONIC.

I texted each person individually to prepare them for how to dress and what to expect. As they arrived, some were jittery, others open-minded, curious and all supportive.

We were all in a large mood lit room in a restful position able to self-meditate as 3 different essential oils were applied to all of us to release stress, promote relaxation and provided a soothing atmosphere. We then all received an acupuncture treatment. For some, this was a first-time experience on all counts. After our journey of what I hoped provided them with a peaceful calm we adjourned back to my home for what I framed in the invitation as delights. You know those things all adults gather to enjoy, good food, drink and company to share with.

As with any good celebration you always provide your attendees with a thank you for coming bag. As children we called them a "goodie bag". You know, it held all the goodies your host wanted to share with you for coming like the craft you made, chocolate, pixie stixs, small toys and well you get the idea. In true form all guests departed with a thank you bag. I filled them with my wellness discoveries over the last few years things like supplements, oils, balms, my seasonal homemade grape jelly and kindness cards. A simple thank you for coming, hope the cards inspire you, the other items remind you to be attentive to your own wellness and my appreciation for sharing in my journey. Yes, to most it was a goodie bag minus the chocolate, pixie stixs and toys.

It wasn't until a week later I decided to reach out to these attendees to ask their experience and thoughts of the event. The responses received noted things such as a good night sleep, slept well, felt more relaxed, the next day I experienced a peaceful calm and it was nice to learn so many new things.

But did they feel my gratitude, and afterward was wellness even apparent?

Attendees

Growing up Italian, I feel my family is very large. To invite all my family, I grew up with alone which now includes very small children would include about 32 people that currently live in 5 states across America. Then I reviewed my Making Moments Matter list and came up with so many more people I wanted to attend this thankfulness & wellness celebration. The process of people to invite like with any event held its own challenges. I'm sure you know that feeling…you're excited about sharing with people, you want to shout it from the roof tops, let everyone know and tell as many people as you can.

You discover something so amazing and you want to share it with everyone you know. Then you settle into circumstances, and well, the reality of it is that it then becomes a cost issue. You need to decide the who, what, where, when and hows that work not only for your end result but your budget.

I narrowed my thinking down to 20 people. The original invitation was sent to both my children with a guest each, all my siblings, a few of my dear friends, my ex-husband, his wife as well as my beau and his children. Included in each invitation was a handwritten note that read:

For me the last year has been filled with many life changing events. As my family you have been there for me in a special way. This is my opportunity to say…thank you. With a shared celebration of wellness for each of us as we move into a new year!

You find as you get older your circle of friends decreases as you only keep dear those who matter to you most. I wanted to invite several others but due to type of event, the time and costs this is where I drew the line. I knew some people may feel uncomfortable, unaware of guest list, my one child was just stationed several states away, others lived far away; I sent invitations regardless of outcome because to me they each mattered in a special way. I wanted them all to feel my thankfulness and appreciation for them in my life regardless.

There was one very dear person in my life that I wanted to attend. Though knowing her state of affairs and distance it would have been an undertaking for something that amounted to 3 hours. Gracefully she understood.

The seven people that attended the event included: one of my children with a guest, my sister and her fiancé, two dear friends and my beau. It was a very intimate gathering.

The Challenge

I decided to send each attendee a survey with a self-addressed stamped envelope assuring the survey would be returned. Along with a challenge, more notably a small task noting this was not in any shape or form a chain letter process.

The survey was simple, a way for attendees to communicate their thoughts, feelings and perception of the thankfulness & wellness night whereas the challenge if taken would be a small commitment on their part.

The survey read:

What was your impression of the thankfulness & wellness celebration?

From your perspective what would you add, remove or change with the event?

Would you attend this annually?

If a fee was involved would you still attend? Yes or No

What fee would suit your budget?

What types of wellness exploration, enlightenment would you consider?

Acupuncture, Chakras, Mediation, Nutrition, Oils, Reiki, Sound, Spiritual, Stones, Yoga   Other

What do you feel a timeframe for such an event should be?

The challenge note read:

Hello…

Thank you for coming to the Thankfulness & Wellness Night.

I hope you were able to discover new methods of wellness and feel the thankfulness & love I have for you being a part of my life.

I hope you choose to take on this challenge…enclosed please find 5 note cards with postage stamps.   If you don't wish to take on this challenge, please keep all the enclosures in memory of me.

Over the course of the next 6 weeks if you feel thankful for someone that has touched your life, past or present, alive or deceased (if deceased no need in applying postage). I ask you to take a moment and send them your thoughts using one of the enclosed note cards. Examples would be...write what you remember of them, or doing with you, how that impacts your life today, why you are thankful they were in your life good or bad...blah, blah, blah you get the idea.

After writing the note card in your own words write the feelings you experienced after completing the note card on the back of the enclosed survey. Note: you may not have any feelings, or you may have tons. This part of the challenge is honestly all individually you.

Then if the recipient (person you sent note card to) responds to you feel free also to jot that on the back on the survey sheet. Now, if you sent this to someone deceased, you may not get a physical response. However, you may see something in upcoming days that reminds you of that person or you talk to someone that brings that person up...this too will be only for you to discern.

Some of your responses to this challenge may include, yet aren't limited to, the following:

The person I sent the first note card to responded to me via text and said...
I never received any feedback from any of the note cards.
I kept the stamps and thought this was a stupid challenge.
Who honestly has this kinda time I just wanta watch television when I have down time.
I'd rather exercise to clear my mind & body of stress then take on any extra stress or emotionality.
Getting in touch with my emotions is not my thing.

I don't see any connection of wellness or thankfulness in this challenge.

And no, I did not do this to keep the post-office in business, this is part of my research on a book I'm writing.

I realize this process may take time so feel free to wait a few months before returning survey in the self-addressed stamped envelope or return the survey at your will with any of your thoughts on the back. I appreciate all your opinions and comments. I can only hope you discover the feeling of thankfulness I have discovered and linked with love.

Hugs,

P.S. This is not a chain letter process...this is simply to see how being thankful one to another generates your emotions and spirit in a positive way. Oh, and by the way you can't send any of the note cards back to me...I'm off limits.

Celebration Results

Chain Letter this is NOT

As a young student in elementary and middle school a popular thing to do was send around a chain letter. You'd receive the letter and would have to give it to a certain number of recipients in a certain time frame anonymously and your wish would come true.

The first time I received a chain letter I had to re-write it in long hand for each person I was going to mail it to. To keep things secret, you never put your return address on it and back then we licked the postage stamps. I think a stamp was about thirteen cents. As you grew up, so did the world, we lived in.

By middle school you no longer had to handwrite the letters. You simply went to the local library and paid one hard-earned quarter for each copy. Rather than mailing it, you slipped it into other students' lockers. As I recall sometimes you just dreaded seeing that folded paper. Honestly, whether it was your time or money, it all added up with very little in the results department. I don't know if we just grew up or if over the years the chain letter has become an ideal of the past.

But a chain letter this process and challenge was not. Making Moment Matter's intent was to truly touch people assuring them not only did they touch another person's life but, for that moment one person to another there was thankfulness. The intention was for the recipients to continue the process but not as a chain letter for wishes of wealth, but as an emotional connection that in a special dynamic way provided each party with euphoria.

Asking the attendees of the thankfulness & wellness celebration was to determine if they experienced the same feelings I did.

Feedback

For myself, as this mission-process unfolded, I discovered my heart open in a more vibrant way. With each photocard that was sent out I was elated with emotion, from the memory and joy that person brought to me in the past to how something they shared with me I still carry within myself, spirit-soul and life.

My hope with the challenge to my 7 attendees was to see if they too received such connection or results.

Three months passed since the Thankfulness and Wellness Celebration. I decided it was time to review the outcome of my attendees. Of the original 7 I had spoken with 5 of my guests who shared their thoughts and received only 2 of the surveys back. The results all varied, based on the individuals.

As far as continuing an actual event the consensus was

positive, the cost for said event amongst attendees varied. All in all, my takeaway was any future wellness event planned should be held as an open house. This format would allow people to come learn about areas of interest for themselves; they could directly schedule a consult based on their individual needs and the functionality would be conducive to all.

It was interesting that all 7 enjoyed learning about the wellness part. They enjoyed the gathering with delights but, it was the reaching out to others and the thankfulness pieces they each found perplexing in their own ways.

One of my dear friends said she sent out all the cards. She acknowledged one of the cards she sent was quite meaningful to her. She then grimaced, as if shocked she never received a response.

My child that attended said, "I wrote the card and it took a day or so but, it opened the line of communication with the receiver." I thought that was a positive outcome.

My sister sent her survey back with plenty of notes. She sent out most of the cards. One went to a close friend there was no response, a family member who cried and was grateful. Another to a relative whose response was thanks. My sister acknowledged that she was glad she went the extra mile sending the card, knowing how it proved her character and integrity. The fourth and final card my sister sent she expected would give her something to express. Yet strangely, the safety card, as I call it, yielded no response. The lack of response seemed to bother my sister more than if she received one. As we spoke, I concluded my sister shared something meaningful and thoughtful in hopes of helping the other person. I explained to my sister that sometimes it's not about you. Your words could have affected that person in a way they didn't want to confront or maybe they choose not to respond because to them your action didn't matter. That's when you let it go and move on. As for the fifth card, she said, "Who knows?" Her final thoughts on how she felt about thankfulness were, "I am grateful for everything in my life. It is very sad that all too often some people give so much of themselves and others don't seem to care. I understand everyone is in a different place in life, but it takes mere moments to express gratitude and appreciation." "For myself, I will continue to be pleasant and give of myself accordingly, but with age I have realized how very few, real important people there are in my world and I am happy with a very small circle!"

My other dear friend said, "that's not how I do things, for now it's on hold, I'll try to do it." When we spoke, she made me realize everyone does things in their own way. To challenge someone to do it the way that worked for you may not be best approach. In time if the idea speaks to that person they can and will do it for themselves.

The final survey I received was from my beau providing very detailed thoughts. For example: to host the event outside to bring together oneself with nature, he referenced wellness like a diet that it needs to be a total change of personal focus and lifestyle, noting if you don't make that shift it's never permanent. He didn't mention anything about the cards. Knowing him, he used the stamps and the cards are tucked away in a drawer somewhere.

My take-away – I was glad for the responses. It shows me you can't always please everyone. People are willing to try new things, experiences teach them to be open for new ideas, that if something someone else does speaks to you and your spirit, you will do it in a way that best suits you.

PART 5
SPIRITUAL FACTOR

Religion...Spirituality

I'm not that person who likes to get all spiritual, or preachy. However, I will tell you when I tried to rationalize the connectivity as a religious-spiritual component I uncovered yet another of my childhood lessons or so it seems now. As my mother longed to discover her spiritual place, my sisters, brother and I were taken along on the expedition. Having been raised in a Roman Catholic Church that was where she began our journey. My sisters, brother and I attended a local Roman Catholic Church where all four of us did receive our holy communion. Though as young children being raised in this religion in a time the world was vastly changing, she did expose us to all religious venues within our community.

We had been active participants in Baptist, Episcopalian, Methodist, Presbyterian, Reformed, and Temple to name a few. It wasn't until I was a teenager, when my mother finally settled on an Evangelical Church because that was where her spirit felt at peace.

Being under her roof, we, for all intent and purposes, were raised as disciples of a multitude of religions. Then when we left our childhood roof it was our choice as to how to cultivate our spiritual path.

My choice for a long time was that of no choice. I claimed to follow whichever suited at that moment. Then as life goes you fall in love and get married. This was a sticky wicket. His family practiced Roman Catholicism and they didn't want us to get married in an Evangelical house of worship. My mother and dad said they wouldn't attend if the wedding was held in a cold concrete church. We were young and honestly not prepared to make a religious decision. That's when my future grandmother said, "I have a friend who's a judge; he can marry you." It was the easy way out or as my mother put it...you got married by a judge on a dance floor.

As our family blossomed, the questions arose. How will you raise the children? What religion will you follow? Yes, I had a strong belief in God, prayed and spoke with him as if he sat next to me but I didn't feel the need to go to a building to worship. I simply wasn't a fan of the symbolism held within religion. My then husband simply didn't practice the religion he was raised with. So, we had forgone religion. Sundays were set as being family time, spending time together.

Unbeknownst to me at the time, as time passes you go through a discovery period where you feel your spirit pull at you. It asks…What will you do in the circumstance? What do you stand for? What do you believe? The time when, how you listen matters as much as your choice to respond and well, that my friend, is all you.

Over the course of the past year I was fortunate to learn some other beliefs such as the Hindi's who worship the "Om", Buddist, Muslim, Jainism and Sikhim. I've come to understand that all these different cultures all have their own belief in the Divine. Some practice their religion while others have a relationship. It is truly your spiritual choice.

You see, religion is a practice of faith where I believe spirituality is your inner relationship with the divine.

"Life is a repeated cycle of getting lost and then finding yourself again. There are many smaller cycles within that cycle where you get lost to a smaller degree and then remember yourself again. Sometimes you do it to yourself on purpose, consciously or unconsciously. Every time you get lost it is so that you can learn something or experience something from a different perspective."
~Jay Woodman

Take a moment and read that statement a few times. Each time I read it I understand it through a different lens.

To each person, the moments that matter change as the cycles of our life change. You discover the moments are like that parable – "The jar of life…rocks, pebbles and sand" …it's a story about priorities or time management you decided. Simply put it goes something like this:

You have a jar into the jar you put rocks just when you think it's filled up you add pebbles. Again, you think it's filled, and you add sand. Each of these elements represent moment you add to your life. Then when you think nothing else can fit in the jar you add water to fill it up. The water is like the extra special moments in your life they bubble up to the top, some overflow and leave other items remain. The beauty of it is what remains in the jar are those moments that matter to you.

For most people the time in our lives goes day by day with no understanding or idea of how the moments affect each other. Then there are those times that come with age or circumstance that make you aware to cherish the moments as your time on this earth is limited.

Every breath is a blessing we take in what our vessel called a body needs. The time spent with others is your time to share life, spirt, soul and you create a difference in both parties mental, physical, spiritual and emotional beings. Then is the goal of sharing love and life mastered.

From the spiritual lens I reason as children we come into this world very connected to our spirit. As we grow and are taught about society and what is expected, we stop listening to our inner voice. At times throughout our lives it alerts us and those are times whether you choose to listen or not. Then as we get older, I believe especially closer to death we reconnect with that spirit. At this stage of life, we know enough to keep silent as to not be thought by our family or society as mentally ill or such. Others stay connected to that sense for most of their lives and cultivate it as they see fit. Hence it becomes our cycle of our life on repeat.

That inner-voice or spirit is always with you. Some of us may never have had the opportunity to hear it, others may have chosen to ignore it, for some it may have been enough that they created a mute button. I'm guessing others have it coming through loud and clear every day that they don't know how to control it and lastly there are those people out there cycling around like a dance with it. No matter where and your inner-voice or spirit are rest assured there comes a point in your life if you choose to listen it not only chaperons you down your path with ease it also allows you to find your purpose and guides you to a more distinct awakening of your true self.

As with any relationship when your awakened to your spirit you build that relationship to transform not only your thinking or feeling but to free yourself of fears.

"Each morning we are born again. What we do today is what matters most." ~ Budda

This mission enabled me to realize that quote from Budda is spot on each day is a new day, we need to rejoice in it, share our love and light. For this practice will sustain our inner spirit.

For me this process has been a mission of the heart.

PART 6
AFTERTHOUGHTS

Random thoughts along the way

This is a random section of thoughts I've jotted down over the course of this venture. Who knows? Maybe one will speak to you.

- I would rather take the time now being present to acknowledge the people, family, friends, colleagues and acquaintances to in essence effect their lives in a positive way for sharing in mine.
- I found this experience very prolific and I have continued, maybe not on a daily basis, sending notes to those people that have moved my spirit.
- Happiness…the more you pick up on the positive around you the better you feel.
- Grateful people are more energetic, emotionally intelligent, forgiving and less likely to be depressed, anxious or lonely.
- For many of us life is a series of events and choices. We start on our road young given a model provided by our family and friends on the things were supposed to do. We seldom realize there was a choice to be made as we seem to be on autopilot going through life. But then "that moment" presents itself…we stop or slow our roll and examine our life. We see missed opportunities, a failed relationship, a broken friendship and though we can't change our past decisions we now have the ability to learn from them. It's at this stage of our life when we re-examine, open our heart to the moment that have carried us to this juncture.
- It wasn't until I finished a year of writing thank yous that I gave myself the time to realize these moments I wrote to individuals about filled my heart, built my integrity, dreams and awakened my spirit again, thus creating the best me.
- I've learned to let the words "appreciate every

moment" resonate within me every day because our time is precious, our love yearns to be shared and no matter how big or small, average or grand our gesture is in that moment, it matters and makes a difference to ourselves and the lives we touch.

• This project of gratitude opened my heart and spirit to see change in life is possible. The sooner we learn to build on the moments, the sooner our lives move in the direction we were intended for.

• To open yourself up to this concept, reflect on your moments, see where you can cherish the past, learn how to move from discontent and build into your future, the sooner, as I see it, you level up your happiness, discover your passion, curiosity, love of life then as you move forward spread joy and when those moments that matter fall upon you rather then wish them by, you embrace them.

• Knowing you were meant to connect with that time, learn from it, accepting the experience and moving forward is profound.

• During this process I learned some moments are meant to stay where they were in time.

• Did you ever think about time? Its like a magical thread that weaves event & lives together. The bigger question is WHY?

• In an effort to minimize my footprint I started cleaning out my home. I noticed I saved clothes remembering a time I may have been thinner or recalling a special event that evoked a memory of a moment that is long gone. I came across a hall pass I was given in my high school years I saved it for more than 35 years. It was from my art teacher. So, in good faith I sent this man the hall pass along with a thank you for his belief in my abilities, providing me encouragement and never letting my creativity be stifled. Funny how life works, people come and go through your life. I recently came in contact with him as his granddaughter went to school where I worked. Now I see how I've been tethered with this man. He was a reflection of time pasted in my life, allowing me to see my dreams and goals as a teenager to where I am now as an adult. I may not have ever achieved that big career I had once wanted but, looking back on the time from then to now, my accomplishments, family and friends have been a far better blessing. Sharing in their lives and having the opportunity to build those relationship far outweigh any power career. I've been fortunate to do so many things that have broadened myself, my abilities and allowed me to spend time with those that mattered to me in my life. The connections with those we love is truly something to be thankful for.

Sharables

Take the time to think of ways you can be thankful or share gratitude throughout your day. You can simply start out by printing the phrases below on a paper and place them in a location or locations you will see it daily, on the frig, mirror in bathroom, on the car dashboard or computer. This will help to keep you mindful.

Today I am Thankful for…

I will do one act of thankfulness today
At the end of the day you write in journal what you were thankful for or whatever your daily act of thankfulness was. Then at any time to lift your spirit you could reflect on that journal and by reading your act on that one day it will fill your emotional bank with joy.

Other ideas that can be sharable recycle a jar of your choosing an emptied and cleaned out mayonnaise container, mason jar or old coffee can. Next to the vessel keep a pen and note pad of sorts. Then every time you pass the jar jot down what you are thankful or grateful for that day it could be as simple as an easy commute to work, someone aided you in a special way, you cherished speaking with an old friend. Then you decide when to open the container and read the notes you added. Maybe after a month, six months or year, no matter when it is you will feel a warmth encapsulate you. That feeling you will want to infect someone else with to bring them the blessings and joys of a thankful heart.

Unsure on creating your own sharable then visit the website for other items such as journals that awaken thankfulness, gratitude and mindfulness, inspirational notecards, copies of the photographs with destination descriptions, affirmation bracelets, wall art, temporary tattoos and more.

YOU

Ask yourself…how do you feel in this moment?
Can you remember sharing any specific time in your life with another person that has given you a lifelong memory?
Would you like to take a simple moment and reach out to that person to let them know?
More importantly are you prepared if they reach back good or bad?
Will you listen to that inner-voice or spirit and trust in its guidance for your life?
Are you prepared to discover a deeper connectivity and understanding of life, light and love?
Are you willing to take a journey to thank you and find where it leads?
Where will your journey of thank you lead to?
What will you discover on your journey?
There are 365 days in a year…How will you use the days in your next year?

There are so many milestones and unforgettable moments in each of our lives moving forward. Let's not just hold those moments dear to our hearts and in our minds but share them.

Spread the thankfulness, peace, joy, laughter, love and light daily to make each of our days better than the last.

What will you decide to do for all your tomorrows?

In the end as my heart filled with thankfulness, I saw this mission as a vehicle that enabled me to do great things to share and show my life, thoughts and hopefully be an inspiration to you.

Now it's your turn go out uncover your journey and always find JOY in it!

PART 7
HELPS & HEALS

RENEE MORAN

Helps...Heals

As I began my journey, I never expected all that would unfold to me in my life and environment around me but also the world we all live in. The first thought of sending a thank you note each day for a year to raise the spirit of people that touched my life turned into a magical passage of awakening myself, my spirit and the world.

In the beginning the notes gave me a few moments of calm, solitude and peace as I chose a picture and wrote a memory or message. As I received responses the thank you notes seemed to provide an uplifting feeling for the receiver as well as I the giver. Which gave me motivation to keep moving forward. Through family setbacks I explored a deeper sense of being through yoga, meditation, acupuncture, oils, sound therapy, and personal development. All those factors combined enabled me to not only help myself, grow spiritually, they offered me a sense of what a simple thank you can achieve.

On my journey to thank you I saw a spark ignited in myself that I hadn't seen in years. I decided I wanted my light to shine using a simple offer of thanks and gratitude that in effect would not only help heal each of us, but it can help heal the world.

Recently our world has globally been under siege from a virus. With people isolating in their homes with limited exposure to the outside world they are wanting to do something to help mankind. This want is our spirit asking to help and heal.

People all over my amazing America have shared resources, retooled factories and children and adults alike are sending virtual thank yous, crafting messages on sidewalk and so much more to share their gratitude and thankfulness to all those helping to heal not only our fellow man but the environment and world we live in.

It has been a blessing for me to see how instinctually people want to spread gratitude and thankfulness to all those people that help us every day. Together we will rise above as we make a conscious decision to choose…Faith over Fear, Peace over Panic, Love over Loneliness, Inspiration over Isolation.

Where are you? I'm traveling through gratitude in the middle of a miracle on my way sharing, my love, light and laughter with the world

THANK YOUS

Thank Yous

To Lynn J. Everard for sharing his truth, supporting and guiding me in the publishing process and believing in my message.

To Lukkas Wolf and Two Wolves Company for their vision and artistic assistance.

To my Godmother, Branch and Betsy for taking the time to proofread, review, criticize, discuss allowing me to expand my thinking, reach and creative muscle.

To Fred if it was not for you letting me leave, I may never have learned the depths of love & life.

To all my parents for educating me not only in life but in death how connected we all are.

To Fallon & Matthew for your support, understanding of my eccentricities, knowing now and forever we will always be housed together within our hearts.

To Greg for believing in me and allowing me to blossom.

Thank you for purchasing this book.
 I hope a little of my sparkle has sprinkled along your life path, that you enjoyed the read,
are inspired to shine your thankfulness, laughter, love and light upon a new day.

ABOUT THE AUTHOR

After attending art school and working briefly in graphic design, advertising and real estate, Renee Moran began a journey of self-discovery to find a medium that would best enable her to share her artistic talents and her unique perspectives with others. Prior to pursuing her education, she was dedicated to her family bringing stability during some troubling times. After art school, she began to find herself and as the mom of two children, she immersed herself in every facet of their lives.

As a photojournalist, Renee found that her ability to tell a story both with photos and words brought her purpose and passion. Sharing both with her community sparked an idea that later bloomed into a year-long mission of "giving thanks."

Renee worked hard to love her children and to keep her creativity alive. It was through her experiences and with the artistic and journalistic influences, she discovered a way to give thanks for her life's journey. She would share with others, the gifts she had received. Her mission "Making Moments Matter" had begun.

The mission was simple yet involved. However, in the end, she found that in order to complete her mission, she needed to share her year-long "Journey to Thank You" with others. As she dispensed hope, love, and gratitude freely, the process opened her heart and mind. Ultimately, it enabled her to share her experience of love, light, beauty, balance, and laughter with those around her.

RENEE MORAN

WHAT ARE YOU GRATEFUL FOR?

I am grateful for_____

_____

_____

_____

_____

_____

_____

_____

_____

_____

_____

_____

_____

_____

_____

_____

WHAT IDEAS DO YOU HAVE TO BRING JOY TO OTHERS?

My ideas_____

_____

_____

_____

_____

_____

_____

_____

_____

_____

_____

_____

_____

_____

_____

_____

_____